Copyright © 2016 by Ricky Gaines

All rights reserved. No part of this publication may be reproduced, distributed, or transmitted in any form or by any means, including photocopying, recording, or other electronic or mechanical methods, without the prior written permission of the publisher, except in the case of brief quotations embodied in critical reviews and certain other noncommercial uses permitted by copyright law. For permission requests, email the publisher at the email address listed below.

Scripture quotation's marked KJV are taken from the King James Version of the bible.

Ordering Information:

Capital Gaines LLC
4023 Kennett Pike #2082
Wilmington, DE 19807
Email: capitallgainesllc@gmail.com
Phone: 415-857-5433
Website: www.capgalnesllc.com
Printed in the United States of America

First Edition Printing, 2016

Ideas More Powerful Than Force/ Ricky Gaines

Ideas More Powerful Than Force

_____

_____

Dedication

This booklet is dedicated to saving a life and empowering someone, somewhere in this world. I hope to inspire you to positively transform - and transcend - your situation and your circumstances.

This booklet is also dedicated to my Lord and Savior Jesus Christ (who is my rock).

To my family (who inspires me every day to be better and to never settle for mediocrity).

To my Team Ricky family - (who continues to stand by my side), and to all of their supporters.

Thank you very much.

I hope you all enjoy it.

To my cousin Chico - until we meet again in the Valley of the Kings - I love you cousin!

This one is for our posterity Brodie!

A minor, but lasting tribute!

I send my royal salutes to you - in spirit and in literary form.

R.G.

"Where the Spirit of the Lord is, there is liberty".

2 Corinthians 3:17 KJV

Table of Contents

1) Dedication — pg. 5

2) Foreword — pg. 7

3) Determined to Pay it Forward. — pg. 8-10

4) The King's Project. — pg. 11-17

5) Adversity, The Mother of Creativity. — pg. 18-23

6) Faith, Purpose & Direction. — pg. 24-26

7) Bonus Section: A Start-up Business Plan Outline. — pg. 27-44

"Paying it Forward Project"

FOREWARD

Many years ago, when Ricky Gaines first shared his visions for the possibilities of his future, It was imminent that this was someone with a deep passion for life. His energy, enthusiasm and confidence just seemed to flow from him. His passion to improve and progress the quality of not only his own life, but the lives of all those around him could not be denied.

Ricky has spoken of writing a book for quite some time, and it was no surprise when he revealed that he had actually completed a first edition booklet.

As you read this booklet you will find within the following pages that it is very moving and inspirational, from personal stories to a time-line of his own life.

Self-help, education and building self-awareness is vital to all of us as a society. Whether you are incarcerated, a stay at home parent, a student, or an entrepreneur - this booklet has something for you.

Ricky has dedicated his life's work to advancing human potential and promoting equality. Over the years we have come to see the work Ricky has done to improve himself, his family and the community.

Many of todays incarcerated-citizens have written books. What makes this one stand out is the rawness of real life, the opportunity to help others and the ability to transcend poverty, crime, and incarceration.

It's clear this is one of Ricky's many creative endeavors and I am sure that there is more to come.

A. Parra
2016

Determined to Pay It Forward!

Photo of Ricky Gaines at his Patten University graduation, San Quentin CA (2010)

    Wow, where do I begin? I guess you have all heard that trouble is a lot easier to get into than to get out of. From the time I heard the metal clang of the prison doors slamming shut, I knew that my journey to get to the other side would not be a walk in the park.

As I lay in bed at night, thoughts flow through my mind about how I landed myself in prison. Not so much about how it affects me, but more importantly thoughts of how it affects other people. For example, the effects it has on my children growing up without a full time father present in the home. Many days and nights spent tossing and turning, remorsefully realizing the heavy impact of my actions on multiple people.

A real eye opener occurred for me when I lost my cousin Chico (2004), who was like my brother, taken away by a violent act of crime. Not to mention, finally understanding the deadly "ripple effect" that my negative actions has on the community. Adding to the statistics of another young, uneducated black man incarcerated in the criminal justice system is the opposite of what the community needs.

Therefore I knew that I had to make a change, and I also had my work cut out for me.

So the first and most consistent thing I could and had the ability to work on was my education. Once I completed my GED (1997), I then worked tirelessly at acquiring my Associates of Arts degree (2010) through Patten University, via Prison University Project (a private nonprofit organization). I continue to strive for my Bachelors Degree in business administration and psychology. Not just for me, but for my family, my community and society as a whole.

Extra special thanks to all the volunteer educators who devoted their time, energy and efforts to helping this cause. I hope by me taking the time to seriously study, seek growth and development through this process that I will be able to articulate my knowledge and understanding to my family, the youth, and members of my community.

Thereby increasing public safety and improving positive out-comes for people in need of positive motivation, encouragement and examples.

Well, as I said at the beginning, trouble is a lot easier to get into than to get out of. Today even though I am not fully out of trouble yet (currently incarcerated), I'm thankful and appreciative because God has helped me to find purpose within this adverse situation. My hope is simply to reach just one person with the message of positive transformation.

"To make a positive difference in the lives of others" has become my life's mission. As a tutor, instructor, and facilitator in several nonprofit volunteer programs, I hope that I am hitting the mark. I tell myself often, "Ricky, if you can reach just one person, if you can stop one relative, friend or stranger in the community from victimizing another community member or from becoming a victim of crime or violence, then Yes, you are definitely hitting the mark of positive transformation that is needed in our society."

My resolve is sure, and I am determined not to allow these hard, and extremely consequential lessons to be a waste of time, tax payers' dollars or any more lives. So I ask you, the reader, to please join me, and let's keep it going.

BE DETERMINED TO PAY IT FORWARD! By Ricky Gaines

Originally written & published in "What I Know Now" (May, 2015),

A Project of Stanford Prisons Volunteer Group. Haas Center for Public Service. Stanford University.

THE KING'S PROJECT

By Ricky Gaines

The King's Project

Uncle Freddy, who is the oldest of Grandma Mattie's eight children, would always jokingly tell me that he had a son my age, and that he could beat me up.

"Lil' Rick, my son Chico is my junior like you are to your Dad, and if I tell him to get on you, he will do it," Uncle Fred would say.

"Well, what's the problem, go and get him," I'd shoot back at my uncle, trying to sound serious. Uncle Freddy loved me and I loved him. He'd always find some creative way for me to go places with him, like to the grocery store, business seminars, or to do odds jobs around the city with him. I think that he felt guilty about not having his son Chico living with him

"Hey son, come and ride with me to Raley's. We need to go buy some barbeque sauce and sodas for Momma," he said on a day when the family was visiting my Grandmother's house for a family gathering. We lived in Pittsburg, California; a small town-city in the Bay Area, near Richmond, where everyone knows each other or their families. Grandma Mattie has four boys and four girls, of which my father is the youngest son. There's Uncle Freddy, Carl (RIP), Marvin (RIP), and Richard. On the girl's side, there's Aunty Mary, Aunty Evonne, Aunty Mallory (RIP), and Aunty Rosie.

Aunty Rosie is what we would call in our family "the famous aunt", because she is a well-known musician, and has lived in Minneapolis, Minnesota at Prince's Paisley Park Estate, while she was a member of his band. "Diamonds and Pearls" was one of the hit songs that made her famous with Prince, so we have always been very proud as a family of her success.

I eventually met my cousin Chico many years later when I moved in with my Grandmother and started junior high school. It was three months into the school year, and as I walked the halls of Central Junior High, all I could think about was that my cousin Chico also went to that school. Classes were in session already, and I was late because the principal had given my grandmother and I a brief orientation of the school. Walking through the halls I was looking inside every classroom I passed hoping to get a glimpse of my cousin. It's funny because actually I didn't really believe I would see him. Then suddenly I saw a face that I didn't immediately recognize, but something in my gut told me by his return stare that I should've known him. I paused, he stood up and we both just stood still staring at each other.

"Rick, is that you, cousin?" he said with a big grin on his face. I just stood there smiling from ear to ear, lost in thought. He looks a lot like me, dark complexion, slim build, and he's handsome, I thought. "Chico, what's up cousin?" I said as I made an open arms gesture with my hands. By this time, he had totally disrupted the classroom's atmosphere of learning, and he was half-way out the door. Greeting me with a solid hand shake and a warm bear hug, I could tell that he was as happy as I was to finally meet him. We were both twelve years of age, and we had so much catching up to do.

Even though he lived on the other side of town, we were inseparable because nothing could keep us away from each other. As we got older, we bought an apartment together and we continued to be inseparable. If you saw me, you saw him, or knew that he'd be arriving soon.

Chico showed me around school that day, introducing me to people he knew as if I was an ambassador from out of the country.

"Ah Mo' dean, this is my cousin who I've been telling you about, Rick'. He's here now so you know that it's on," he'd say. I didn't have a clue who any of these people were, but I could tell that they were checking me out, and trying to size me up. "Robin, this here is my cousin Rick, he's in your homeroom class, so make him feel comfortable okay?" he said to this pretty young lady with a tremendous smile on her face. She didn't say a word, just kept smiling. I'm looking and smiling first, but after a few minutes, the young lady was still smiling, and now I'm thinking to myself this girl is crazy! Therefore, I eased on down the hall, nodding to my cousin to bring his butt on.

That day in junior high school was like the first day of a brand new life for both of us. Our bond was unbreakable from that moment on, because I think we were anticipating meeting one another and coming together. People were always mentioning me to him, or him to me, and we hadn't even seen each other yet. So the build-up to the moment we met was huge, and we both couldn't wait. I'll never forget the day when I was called into the captain's office while incarcerated in Solano State Prison.

"Mr. Gaines, your sister called and I'm sorry to inform you that your brother had an accident," he said, trying to measure his words. I was not even registering what he was saying, because I knew that I didn't have any brothers. (At least I thought I didn't at the time. I love you Brodie Cornelius.)

"Apparently your brother took a trip to the NBA All-Star game, and there was an accident later that night. Your brother Fredrick Gaines was shot once in the stomach and later died at the hospital," the captain announced, this time looking intently at me, checking for my reactions to his words. In my mind, at first I was thinking that someone back home must have really wanted me to call home, so they had called to the prison with a bogus story about a brother I never had. Then when I heard the name "Fredrick Gaines" my heart dropped to my stomach, and now I began to shake my head as if to say, "You cannot be correct, that's not true. I had just spoken with my cousin Chico nearly a week ago on the phone, and he was happy about his music career which was apparently taking off for him, and he was happily expecting another baby girl." I didn't move, just stood there looking at this person who I had never seen before, telling me about my cousin, like he knew both of us. I wanted to get out of that office as fast as I could, so I turned away, feeling the tears welling up in my eyes.

"I need to get on the telephone sir," I said as I looked back at the captain. I didn't wait for a response as I started out of his office and began walking back to my housing unit. Outside, the air was cool and the night was clear. It seemed like I was walking outside of my body because I could see myself moving at a steady pace but could also feel my eyes burning from the tears.

Memories began to flash into my mind, of my cousin and I, and I began to replay conversations we had over the years in my head. The first time we met came rushing back into my mind.

It seems like so many lives have been touched by my cousin and I, and it's not the same without him around. I dialed the number to my sister's house, but when she answered and accepted the collect call, the sound of her voice took away my breath. I could not even speak. My sister understood the emotions I was consumed by, so she talked and talked, filling me in to every last detail. I was saddened and angered by my cousin's untimely death, because he had totally changed his life and was being a responsible father, making music for a living, and staying away from the streets.

To think that he went to a public event like the NBA All-Star Game and was murdered by some person who shot into a crowd of people just makes me mad at the senselessness of urban violence. His murder is still unsolved.

This tragedy taught me lessons that I can never forget about life, about appreciating opportunities, and about breaking the cycle of crime and violence.

I hope to eventually build a nonprofit corporation for youth and adults who have been affected by gun violence, incarceration, and crime in my cousin's honor. This tragedy happened in April of 2004, and Chico was 28 years of age.

By Ricky Gaines (edited version 2015)

Originally written & published in "Is It Safe?" (2006)

A Prison University Project publication

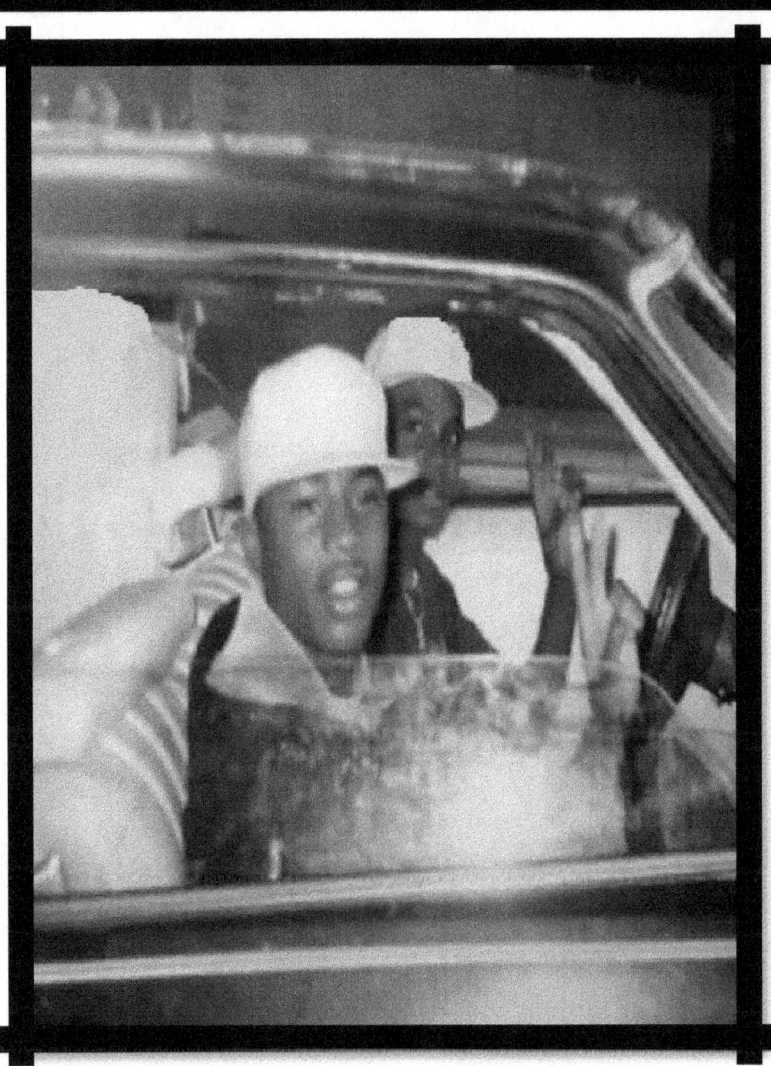

Photo of, Ricky Gaines & Chico Gaines in front of Pittsburg High School, Age 17. "1993"

Adversity, The Mother of Creativity.

Volume 1.

Ricky Gaines is 39 years old and he grew up in Pittsburg, California. For him, life was tough.

Today, Ricky's passion for community organization, social justice advocacy, youth outreach, entrepreneurship, and obtaining a M.B.A (Masters in Business Administration) keeps him full of activity and vigorously engaged in positive actions.

Life Experience:

1976: (May) Born in Pittsburg, California to parents Geraldine & Richard, Ricky is a California - Bay Area native.

1982: Early traumatic exposure - At the age of 6, Ricky's mother was brutally attacked, and shot five times, in a cruel & callous domestic violence abuse incident.

Adversity, The Mother of Creativity.

1994: (May) While his fellow classmates were preparing for graduation, at the age of 18, Ricky became the proud father of a beautiful baby girl, (Rickiesha).

1995: (February) Ricky found out that trouble was a lot easier to get into than to get out of when he was arrested, and charged with robbery/homicide.

1995: (May) While preparing for the fight of his life, (The State of California vs. RICKY), and just 13 days before his 19th Birthday, Ricky became the proud father of a second beautiful baby girl, (Tierra), who was in her mother's womb at the time of Ricky's arrest.

1995: (July) Again, Ricky found out that trouble was a lot easier to get into than out of when he was convicted by a jury, and later given a sentence of 29-years-to-Life (with the possibility of parole), for a drug related robbery and homicide.

1996: (January) At the age of 19, Ricky was sent to San Quentin State Prison (4 Months before his 20th Birthday).

1996: (February) After nearly 30 days, in San Quentin's reception center, Ricky was sent to a newly built maximum security High Desert State Prison, in Susanville, California.

Adversity, The Mother of Creativity.

1997: In spite of residing in one of the most volatile & violent environments imaginable (A Level 4 prison), Ricky was determined to transform his life. Thus, he studied consistently and passed his GED exam the first time taking it. Earning his GED was a tremendous confidence builder, and it lead to further achievements.

1999: (October) Granted a Level - 3 override, Ricky was sent to Solano State Prison, a Level 3 maximum security prison. Less security and more opportunities to grow and develop academically and vocationally.

2001: Ricky earned a vocational trade in Silk Screen Printing. (A Marketable skill.)

2004: Ricky's best friend, his cousin Chico, was murdered by an act of violence.

2005: As a result of good institutional behavior, Ricky's custody was lowered as he was sent to San Quentin State Prison's Level 2 general population.

2005: Ricky got enrolled in Patten University at San Quentin.

2006: Ricky became a tutor for adults, via Robert E. Burton Adult School.

Adversity, The Mother of Creativity.

2007: Ricky became a member of R.E.A.L Choices, a non-profit organization that focuses on Youth Intervention.

2008: Ricky became a member of NO MORE TEARS!, a non-profit organization that focuses on violence prevention.

2009: Ricky got married to his wife, who he's known since junior high school.

2009: One week after getting married, Ricky became a grandfather to a beautiful baby girl, Ki'ajeah.

2010: Ricky received his AA degree from Patten University through the Prison University Project.

2010: Ricky became a member of ALLIANCE FOR C.H.A.N.G.E., a nonprofit organization that focuses on social justice and prisoner reintegration (2010-2016).

2014: (March) Ricky moved his daughter- (Tierra,18) to another state, due to negative realities in California. His goals were simply to love, encourage, and motivate her to earn a high school diploma or GED.

2014: (March) Ricky became a grandfather to a beautiful baby girl, for the second time, (Ki'Chet).

Adversity, The Mother of Creativity.

2014: (June) Ricky moved his other daughter - (Rickiesha, 20) to another state, due to negative realities in CA. His goal was to simply to love, encourage, and motivate her to earn a high school diploma or GED.

2014: (November) Ricky's daughter (Tierra, 19) earns her GED, and gets hired at a new job within the same week.

2015 (January) Ricky's daughter (Rickiesha, 20) earns her GED, and gets hired at the same company that her sister (Tierra) was employed at.

2016: (January) Became the author of "Ideas more Powerful Than Force, Volume 1."

Photo of Ricky and his daughters and granddaughter.

Photos of Ricky's children and grandchildren

Faith, Purpose & Direction.

Hope in becoming a returned citizen.

I have hope that I will become a returned citizen because of my faith in Jesus Christ, and the grace and mercy that He has shown to me.

In the Bible, Jeremiah 29:11 KJV states, "FOR I KNOW THE THOUGHTS THAT I THINK TOWARD YOU, SAITH THE LORD, THOUGHTS OF PEACE AND NOT OF EVIL, TO GIVE YOU AN EXPECTED END."

Therefore, I am Hopeful in my faith and in the word of my Lord and Savior, which promises me a future and a hope.

However I know that faith alone is not enough.

James 2:17 states, "EVEN SO FAITH, IF IT HATH NOT WORKS, IS DEAD, BEING ALONE."

And again, James 2:26 further states, "FOR AS THE BODY WITHOUT THE SPIRIT IS DEAD, SO FAITH WITHOUT WORKS IS DEAD ALSO."

That being said, I know that it is a combination of my faith and my works that will ultimately help me to achieve "the return citizen status" that my family and I hope and pray for.

Faith, Purpose & Direction.

Twenty years ago, I was an at-risk teenager, who dropped out of school at the age of seventeen, became a teen parent at the age of eighteen, and ended up in prison with a 29-year-to-life sentence for a drug related homicide, when I was eighteen.

Today, I am 39 years old, equipped with a GED, an Associate's of Arts Degree, and thousands of hours of training, in social-psychology, early childhood development, criminal justice theory, anger management, substance abuse, parenting education, community justice, restorative justice (just to name a few), and much more experience with making pro-social choices and decisions. I have vowed to live a law-abiding and socially acceptable life.

My desire is to make amends for my poor choices in the past, which is why I give back by volunteering, mentoring, and tutoring at-risk teens and young adults through multiple memberships in community based nonprofit organizations while in prison.

Today, I am positively networking and building alliances with family and friends who are hopeful that ("God Willing") I will become a "returned citizen" in the near future, and hopeful that I will be an asset and a blessing to myself, my family, and to society.

Every day, I am exercising my faith and my works, by continuing to take college classes, continuing to take self-help classes, continuing to attend church services, continuing to volunteer my time, knowledge and effort to helping at-risk teens, adults and whoever else is receptive to the positive changes that I am an advocate for.

By participating in educational and spiritual programs like: *The Last Mile (entrepreneur & tech program), The Alliance for Change (social justice course), No More Tears (violence prevention workshops), The Garden Chapel Church Services (Christian workshop & fellowship), and R.E.A.L. Choices (youth mentorship program)* and learning from them, while incarcerated, I trust that I am placing myself on the road to success, empowerment and responsibility. Making sound choices and decisions day-to-day are the results of applying the knowledge and wisdom gained from various classes, services and workshops. It is an on-going journey, with daily prayers for forgiveness and redemption, and the work will not stop once I am a returned citizen.

I just take it one day at a time, and I am hopeful that when I am a returned citizen, I will be an asset and no longer a liability to myself, my family, and to society. The transition requires good individual and collective support. So, if you are able, and, you wish to support the cause, please contact me for more information on how you can help.

By Ricky Gaines.

Showing the love and paying respects

Photo of Ricky's daughters, Rickiesha & Tierra, with a surprise visit from cousin Chico Gaines. "2003"

Bonus Section:

Forward Progress Project

7. Bonus Section:

A Start-up Business Plan Outline:

Below are a few details of a business plan outline for a potential start-up company, created by Ricky titled, "Forward Progress Project", which will be a 501[c](3) nonprofit corporation when it was formulated.

www.forwardprogressprj.com

Mission Statement of the company:

Our mission is to Break The Cycle of intergenerational incarceration by tutoring, mentoring, and supporting at-risk teenagers and young adults to become productive and law-abiding members of society.

Clients and Students:

Forward Progress Project will serve clients and students who are between the ages 13 to 25.

Goal:

To help students and clients to earn their high school diploma or a GED

Forward Progress Project

www.forwardprogressprj.com

A 501 {c}(3) Nonprofit Corporation

FOUNDER,

Ricky Gaines II.

*not an actual company

pending sponsor/governmental approval

Coming soon… to a city near you.
Forward Progress Project
A (Potential) 501 [c](3) nonprofit corporation
Founder, RICKY GAINES , II.

1.1 Table of Contents

1.0	Cover page	Page 1
1.1	Table of Contents	Page 2
2.0	Executive Summary	Page 3
3.0	Mission Statement	Page 5
4.0	Description of Services	Page 6
5.0	Outreach and Promotion	Page 10
6.0	Finances and Sponsors	Page 13
7.0	Students and Clients	Page 15
8.0	Selection of Staff Procedures	Page 16
9.0	Appendix	Page 18

Appendix not included in booklet.

2.0 Executive Summary pg.3

Ricky became interested in creating "Forward Progress Project" for teens and young adults beginning in 2006 when he served as a teaching assistant and tutor for adults studying to pass the GED or High School Equivalency Exam, in the Robert E. Burton Adult School.

Ricky became inspired once more to create a Forward Progress Project venture in 2007 when he became a mentor to at-risk teenagers, as a member of R.E.A.L. Choices, a California nonprofit corporation which services youth in several bay area counties.

Forward Progress Project will be a company that offers a customized curriculum and course of instruction online, de-signed to prepare clients and students to pass the GED or High School Equivalency exam.

Our Forward Progress curriculum will cover the five core subjects pertaining to the GED or High School Equivalency exam; language arts reading, writing, social studies, science and mathematics.

2.0 Executive Summary continued   4

We will offer a customized curriculum online, and through our mobile application that students and clients can utilized to directly interact with their tutor/mentor at their appointed time. (Please see appendix exhibit 2-A, for courses offered).

Since seventy percent of first-time prisoners who enter a correctional institution does not have a GED or high school diploma, we believe by helping our clients and students pass the GED or High School Equivalency exam, we will also be reducing their chances of being incarcerated.

In addition to earning their diploma, Forward Progress will also provide an incentive package to help create opportunities for students and clients to secure employment and enroll in community college.

Forward Progress Project is not just a community-based business model, it has proven strategies that have been utilized in Ricky's own home and today Ricky's daughters are GED graduates.

3.0 Mission Statement

The mission of "Forward Progress" is to break the cycle of intergeneration incarceration by tutoring, mentoring, and supporting teenagers and young adults to become productive and law-abiding members of society.

4.0 Description of Services 6

4.0 THE SERVICES

We will provide several courses that range from 4, 8, 12, and 16 weeks. (Please see Exhibit - 2A "Courses Offered" in Appendix.)

We utilize "Skype", "Face-Time" and "Google Lounge" to provide live, interactive tutorial sessions to students and clients.

Each course requires 3 online tutorial meetings per week.

Online tutorial sessions are 45 minutes each.

A "Forward Progress You Tube" Channel will be created, which will host video tutorials that are synchronized with students' and clients' meeting schedules and assignments.

A series of lesson-specific tutorial DVD's will be available on the official website.

We will also offer an "Off-Line Public Meeting Option" where (after signing various consent forms) students or clients can meet with Tutors and Mentors at

Public Libraries, Youth Centers, and Schools for face-to-face and group tutoring and mentoring sessions.

4.0 Description of Services - continued 7

The Forward Progress Project offers high quality Mentors and Tutors:

[1] Who are examined and confirmed by law enforcement.

[2] Who are certified by Forward Progress' 16 week youth training course, which prepares all staff members for tutoring and mentoring youth and young adults.

[3] Who are continuously and professionally training in sociology, psychology, child development, criminal justice theory, anger management, substance abuse, community justice, restorative justice, etc.

[4] Who are approved and certified by educational professionals.

[5] Who are private citizens, professionals, and formerly incarcerated citizens who have successfully reintegrated into society.

[6] Who are mature, experienced, and qualified instructors and advisors to youth and young adults.

[7] Who are trustworthy, compassionate, and committed to helping youth and young adults to becoming productive citizens.

***Due to the sensitive nature of Forward Progress' business, we are prohibited from hiring persons convicted of sexual crimes, or persons convicted of a crime against a minor.

4.0 Description of Services - continued   8

Getting Started...

After a brief questionnaire and a formal enrollment application Forward Progress does the following:

Administers an age and grade level appropriate survey and assessment test.

Choose a course of study for the student, based on the results of the assessment test and survey.

Develop a personalized education and mentorship plan for the student, complete with meeting schedule and assignments.

Link the student, with a compatible tutor and mentor, who is responsible for each online session with the student (which consists of a 45 minute session, three times a week).

Provide periodic check-ins (bi-weekly) by our program administrators or our executive director, to proactively trouble-shoot any challenges or issues that may arise.

4.0 Description of Services - continued 9

Employ a merit-based procedure for our top scoring students who score at the top 20% of Practice Test exams.

These Students are considered "ready" to take the official GED or High School Equivalency exam, and they qualify to receive the Exam Financial Fee from Forward Progress.

Forward Progress will pay for these students to take the official exam at an accredited education institution.

5.0 Outreach and Promotion   10

Forward Progress Project recruits students and clients through direct outreach and word-of-mouth promotions.

Most of Forward Progress Project's students and clients will learn about their services through:

1.) Church Congregations.

2.) School Institutions.

3.) Direct Outreach from a Forward Progress Project staff member, and door-to-door promotion.

4.) An acquaintance: each-one, reach-one, and teach-one.

5.) Through social media forms, such as Facebook, Twitter, etc.

Forward Progress Project plans to visit churches, school districts, charter schools, juvenile justice agencies, foster homes, group homes, and homeless shelters.

Forward Progress Project plans to go to youth centers, youth events, and communities of youth and recruit *Youth Ambassadors*, by employing a *Teen Leader Identifier* strategy-which identifies and recruit's teen leaders to participate in our educational and social program.

5.0 Outreach and Promotion

By supporting these teen and young adult leaders - to excel and achieve educational and social success (an earned GED or High School diploma, a legitimate job, and personal empowerment), it will demonstrate the effectiveness of Forward Progress Project's programs, and it will encourage and invite other teens and young adults to partake in the services offered by Forward Progress Project. Students and clients will inspire and empower each other.

Forward Progress Project will also utilize an active Blog webpage on its website.

The blog will have a "Monthly Reviews" feature, where stories of Teens, Mentors, Tutors, Donors and Public Figures are posted and shared monthly for audiences to view and comment.

Stories will articulate how these individuals have faced complex challenges and adversity. Including, how they've succeeded and failed in the past, how they are resiliently bouncing back and succeeding today, and what they plan to do with their newly acquired education and social skills in the future.

We hope the story-telling process will be encouraging, motivating and empowering.

5.0 Outreach and Promotion-continued

Forward Progress Project will make use of sponsor endorsement.

At some point in the process, the live tutorial sessions will be interrupted for a surprise guest speaker, such as a superstar, public figure and or a celebrity. A 15-30 minute speech of encouragement from a celebrity who endorses education and a productive lifestyle, will motivate and engage our students to achieve their educational goals.

Forward Progress Project will also make use of our high-quality incentive package.

(Pending Sponsor Approval)

1. A $500 scholarship, and staff assistance with community college enrollment.
2. A women business skirt/pant suit; A men suit, tie, and a pair of shoes.
3. A $100 gift card.
4. A pair of Nike shoes. (or Reebok, Adidas, etc.)
5. Paid 3-month internship with a Local Business.

6.0 Finances and Sponsors   13

Forward Progress Project will subcontract with a credentialed Teacher, who will serve as it's Education Specialist.

This person's job is to ensure that all Forward Progress Project's curriculum meets State standards, is current and compatible with the content of the new GED and High School Equivalency exam.

This person also ensures that the curriculum is complimentary with local school districts age and grade-level proficiency standards.

Forward Progress Project seeks sponsors and partnerships with corporations, sports teams, juvenile justice agencies, church organizations, school districts, and community centers, but we are not limited to these sponsors and partners.

Forward Progress Project aims to receive donations to build and operate their official website and App.

Forward Progress Project will receive tax-deductible donations to spread the word through direct outreach to the community. **(Pending Approval of a 501[c](3) Tax Exempt Status.)**

6.0 Finances and Sponsors - continued

Forward Progress Project also aims to receive donations of computer equipment, smart mobile phones, business suits, business skirts, shoes, sports tickets, and Nike, Adidas, Reebok, or Under Armour sports gear.

Forward Progress Project aims to receive funding from public and private grants.

Forward Progress Project aims to generate revenue from contracts for post-release education services for recently released juvenile and young adult offenders who do not have a GED or High School Diploma.

Forward Progress Project aims to generate revenue from official merchandise.

7.0 Students and Clients

Forward Progress Project serves students and clients who are between the ages of 13 through 25.

8.0 Selection of Staff Procedures   16

Forward Progress Project's staff selection procedures ensures that all Tutors and Mentors have been examined and confirmed by a law-enforcement official.

For formerly incarcerated citizens: Participants must have their Central File (C-File) examined by a law-enforcement official and a program staff member: (1) to confirm that they are not convicted of a sexual crime, (2) to confirm that they are not convicted of a crime against a minor.

Tutors and Mentors are private citizens, professionals, and formerly incarcerated citizens who have successfully reintegrated into society.

Tutors and Mentors must participate in a vigorous 16 week "Forward Progress Project Training Course", which prepares and certifies our staff for up to 18 months to work with "At-Risk" youth.

Tutors and Mentors must qualify by having academic and rehabilitative credentials, that are verified by Forward Progress Project's staff administrators, such as GED certificates, college classes, vocational trade, and additional training if necessary.

45

CALIFORNIA LEGISLATURE

CERTIFICATE OF RECOGNITION

Ricky Gaines, Jr
Prison University Project

In celebration of your completion of the Associate of Arts degree; and in recognition of your unwavering commitment in continuing your education. May you continue to strive for your Bachelor degree and become an inspiration for those around you.

Assemblyman Tom Ammiano
13th Assembly District
September 7, 2010

A PORTION OF THE PROCEEDS FROM EACH BOOKLET SOLD WILL GO TOWARDS THREE SPECIFIC CAUSES:

(1.) PAYING IT FORWARD PROJECT:

We aspire to provide 25 students or one classroom with backpacks, including school supplies.

(2.) VICTIM & SURVIVOR ASSISTANCE PROJECT:

Our goals are to support the needs of survivors of crime and violence - in whatever manner we can. We hope to become part of the solution, and not a part of the problem.

(3.) EDUCATION & WRITING PROJECT

Provide books, necessities, and educational materials to Ricky.

For more information
contact us @
Capital Gaines LLC
4023 Kennett Pike #2082
Wilmington, DE 19807
Email: capitallgainesllc@gmail.com
Phone: 302-433-6777
Website: www.capgainesllc.com
Printed in the United States of America

Available Now...
@www.amazon.com

SLICK-G PRESENTS: It's Hard Being The Same. By Eric Curtis

SLICK-G PRESENTS: Roxxy. By A.C. Bellard

Ideas More Powerful Than Force. By Ricky Gaines II

SLICK-G PRESENTS: Neologic Thought. By Ah'Khemu

Coming Soon...

SLICK-G PRESENTS: Street Karma by Leo Fountila IV

SLICK-G PRESENTS: Only A Chosen Few by Mack Malik

✫ ✫ ✫ ✫ ✫ ✫ ✫ ✫ ✫ ✫ ✫ ✫ ✫ ✫ ✫ ✫ ✫ ✫ ✫ ✫

For ordering info please visit our website or call
www.capgainesllc.com –302-433-6777

CAPITAL GAINES LLC
4023 Kennett Pike #2082
Wilmington, Delaware 19807
www.capgainesllc.com
Telephone: (415-857-5433)
Email: cg@capgainesllc.com

MAIL PAYMENT TO:

CAPITAL GAINES LLC
4023 Kennett Pike #2082
Wilmington, Delaware 19807

ORDER YOUR BOOKS AND HAVE THEM DELIVERED QUICKLY

MONEY ORDERS/ INSTITUTIONALIZED CHECKS ACCEPTED

TITLE OF BOOK	QUANTITY EACH	TOTAL QUANTITY	METHOD OF PAYMENT	PRICE EACH	TOTAL PRICE
IDEAS MORE POWERFUL THAN FORCE				$15.00	
SLICK-G PRESENTS: IT'S HARD BEING THE SAME				$15.00	
SLICK-G PRESENTS: ROXXY				$15.00	
SLICK-G PRESENTS: TRIUMPH				$10.00	
SLICK-G PRESENTS: NEOLOGIC THOUGHT				$10.00	
SLICK-G PRESENTS: STREET KARMA				$15.00	
SLICK-G PRESENTS: ONLY A CHOOSEN FEW				$15.00	
TOTAL					

SHIP TO:

NAME:
ADDRESS:
CITY/STATE/ZIP CODE:
PHONE:
EMAIL:

FROM:

NAME:
ADDRESS:
CITY/STATE/ZIP CODE:

www.ingramcontent.com/pod-product-compliance
Lightning Source LLC
Chambersburg PA
CBHW051949160426
43198CB00013B/2365